rice cooker creations

40 simple recipes by Zojirushi

ZOJIRUSHI

contents

recipes

a meal-making machine

Almost half the world's population makes the ancient grain a staple in their diets. It is nutritious, inexpensive, versatile, and easy to store and cook. Today, we in the United States are eating more and more of this cholesterol- and gluten-free food—which is low in sodium, very low in fat, and rich in complex carbohydrates, vitamins, and minerals. What's more, unhulled (a.k.a. brown) rice is an excellent source of dietary fiber.

Eating more rice means cooking more rice in our own kitchens. The major problem with cooking rice at home is that most gas or electric stove burners do not turn down to a true simmer. So when the rice has finished boiling and it's time to steam the grains over a small, steady heat source, most people end up burning, or at best, scorching their rice. They either misjudge when to turn down the heat source or they cannot turn the burner down low enough to steam the rice. Instead, they end up boiling it.

In the U.S.—where parboiled, dehydrated rice, frozen rice-in-a-bag, or rice cooked "pasta-style," with lots of water that is later drained off, is often the norm—people marvel at the delicious taste, fragrant aroma, and perfect texture of rice served in Asian restaurants and homes. They wonder why they cannot duplicate that perfect rice in their own kitchen. The answer they seek, the real "secret" to perfect, foolproof rice, is not the cook, but rather, the electric rice cooker.

Rice cooking traditionally calls for measuring X amount of rice and X amount of water and heating them together for X amount of time. Rice cookers, also called rice steamers, make this deceptively simple process really, truly, and reliably simple by handling all the Xs. A cook measures the amount of rice and fills water to the water level line corresponding to the amount of rice, puts it inside the automated counter top appliance, and pushes a button to turn the device on. The rice cooker heats the rice and water until all the water has either been absorbed or evaporated. The rice cooker takes its cues from the boiling water, which maintains a constant temperature (212°F or 100°C, at sea level). Once cooking completes and the water is absorbed by the rice, the temperature change signals the device to keep the rice warm and ready to serve for several hours. With an automated rice cooker, burned grains on the bottom of a pot are almost impossible. Scorched rice is history.

Speaking of history, rice cookers owe their history to the Japanese, for whom rice cooking is a serious art. From its early development in the 1950s, the basic electric rice cooker has become increasingly more advanced, with the introduction of microcomputerization, which allows for multiple cooking settings for multiple types of rice, as well as other grains and foods.

In Japan, the word for cooked rice is also the word for meal. It follows then that rice cookers are also meal cookers. So, we home cooks benefit from rice cookers' ever-advancing ability to serve up perfectly hot, fluffy rice. But we may benefit even more from the devices' versatility in cooking, not only every rice dish we can shake a wooden spoon at, but also non-rice recipes. Rice cookers also cook hot cereals, desserts, soups, and stews, as well as poach fruits, and steam vegetables and meats. Think of it: An entire meal in just one pot.

rice cookers

Conventional Rice Cooker

First invented in 1955, conventional electric rice cookers are inexpensive and ideal for beginners. To cook white rice, all you do is add rice, water, and push a button. Though conventional rice cookers were designed to make perfect white rice, they also excel in making brown and sushi rice with just a few adjustments. Also, because these conventional rice cookers are designed to simply heat, boil, and turn themselves off, they double as convenient steamers. This makes conventional rice cookers the ideal kitchen appliance for those with little kitchen counter space. Preparing a meal has never been this easy.

HOW IT WORKS:

If you take out the inner cooking pan and look inside the main body of the rice cooker, you will see a small round disk, about 1½ inch in diameter, in the center of the heating plate. This is a thermal sensing device, known as a magnetic thermostat, and it sits on a small spring.

When you place rice and water into the inner cooking pan and nestle it into the main body of

the rice cooker, the weight of the inner cooking pan depresses the thermal sensor. With the rice cooker plugged in and the Cook button turned on, the heating plate begins to heat up, bringing the liquid in the inner cooking pan to a boil. Water boils at 212°F, and no higher. So as long as there is water in the pan, the rice cooker will continue to cook. When the rice absorbs all the water, the temperature will begin to rise, since there isn't any water left in the pan. When the thermal sensor senses that the temperature has risen above 212°F, the machine turns off the heater automatically and switches to the "Keep Warm" mode. It's as simple as that!

Micom Rice Cooker

MICOM RICE COOKER

Micom or microcomputerized rice cookers are easily recognizable by their digital face. Equipped with a computer chip, micom rice cookers are ideal for health-conscious brown rice eaters or future home sushi chefs because of their multiple menu selections. The computer chip allows the rice cooker to "think" and adjust cooking lengths and temperatures according to the selected menu, so it not only makes perfect white rice, but also flawless brown rice, sushi rice, and porridge! Unlike with conventional rice cookers, soaking and steaming time before and after cooking rice is automatically programmed, so you don't have to worry about it. Additionally, the timer function allows you to delay the completion, so you can prepare the rice earlier in the day, and not worry about it until it's served at dinner. Because of its added features, the micom rice cooker makes life easier for exacting rice eaters.

HOW IT WORKS:

The top-of-the-line Zojirushi micom rice cooker is the **Neuro Fuzzy®**, a registered trademark name coined by Zojirushi to indicate a rice cooker that uses "fuzzy logic" technology. The micom's fuzzy logic brain does more than simply switching on and off in reaction to temperature. Rather, the rice cooker now fine-tunes temperature and cooking time according to the thermal sensor's calculations. So you can program your rice to be hard or soft, dry or watery, as in the case of rice porridge, the Asian comfort food. You can also program for cooking white, brown, or sweet (glutinous) rice.

IH RICE COOKER

The Induction Heating (IH) System rice cooker introduces a whole new way of cooking rice. Instead of having a heating element at the bottom of the rice cooker to heat the inner cooking pan, it uses induction-heating principles to generate heat within the inner cooking pan. This method also allows rice to cook quickly at a very high temperature, which is not possible with conventional electric or micom rice cookers.

HOW IT WORKS:

The heating method known as Induction Heating (IH) occurs when a magnetic material is placed in a magnetic field. In Zojirushi's case, coils within the bottom of the rice cooker create the magnetic field. When the special two-ply, inner cooking pan (nonstick coated aluminum with stainless steel outer lining) is placed into the rice cooker and the unit is turned on, a magnetic field is generated to create instant heat. Through this technology, the whole inner cooking pan itself becomes the heat source, utilizing both high heat and finely tuned heat adjustments to control the cooking process. The results? Higher and quicker heat response that's more evenly distributed for perfectly cooked rice every time!

WHICH IS THE RIGHT RICE COOKER FOR ME?

The right rice cooker depends on the need and frequency of use by the user. Some of the questions to ask are:

- Do you cook rice often?
- Do you eat brown rice more often than white rice?
- Do you eat/cook hot cereal?
- Do you need a timer function to ensure your rice is ready when you get home from work or wake up in the morning?

If you answer "yes" to any of these questions, a micom rice cooker would be a smart choice with its brown rice and porridge functions, timer, and other features. If you don't need all that, an electric rice cooker would be just fine. If you want all that and the best-tasting rice in town, we recommend the top-of-the-line IH rice cooker.

WHAT ARE ALL THOSE FEATURES?

Zojirushi's higher-end models are very sophisticated, and can do a lot of things. Here are the features available on some of our rice cookers.

LCD Display: Conveniently displays clock and/or timer. Large color LCD display is easy to read.

Automatic Keep Warm: Keep warm system automatically activates after cooking completes in order to keep rice tasting fresh for an extended period. The keep warm temperature is approximately 160°F.

Extended Keep Warm: The rice is kept warm at a slightly lower temperature (approx. 140°F) than Automatic Keep Warm to reduce dryness, discoloration, or odor. (Returns to Automatic Keep Warm after 8 hours.)

Reheating Cycle: Reheats the kept warm rice from Extended Keep Warm or cold rice to the perfect serving temperature.

Timer: Timer function ensures cooked rice by a set time.

Nonstick Interior: Durable nonstick coating prevents rice from sticking and makes cleaning fast and easy.

Menu Settings: Provides selection of different menus that correspond to different cooking times and temperatures.

9

tips & techniques

SHORT GRAIN
Short grain rice has a short, plump, almost round kernel. Cooked grains are soft and cling together.

MEDIUM GRAIN
Medium grain rice has a shorter, wider kernel (two to three times longer than its width) than long grain rice. Cooked grains are more moist and tender, and have a greater tendency to cling together than long grain.

LONG GRAIN
Long grain rice has a long, slender kernel, four to five times longer than its width. Cooked grains are separate, light, and fluffy.

ARBORIO
U.S. Arborio rice is large, bold rice with a characteristic white dot at the center of the grain. By the way of length/width ratio and starch characteristics, it is classified as medium grain rice. Primarily used in risotto, this rice develops a creamy texture around a chewy center and has exceptional ability to absorb flavors.

BROWN RICE
Rice that has only its outermost husk removed. It is nutritious and delicious, and perfect for those living a healthy lifestyle. To cook brown rice, it helps to have a rice cooker with a brown rice menu option, which cooks the rice at a lower temperature longer to penetrate the tough bran, resulting in delicious brown rice.

STORING RICE
You may store white and wild rice at room temperature for an indefinite period. After a month, store brown and specialty rice in the refrigerator in a sealed container. Cooked rice may be stored in the fridge for up to five days. Store cooked rice in the freezer for six to eight months in plastic freezer bags. If you buy a variety of rice in bulk, be sure to label them when you place in smaller storage containers, as different-grained rice are difficult to distinguish from one another.

MEASURING RICE
It is important to measure rice accurately using the rice measuring cup that comes with every Zojirushi rice cooker. This is a measuring cup specifically designed to measure rice and cook in the rice cooker. Level off with a knife or chopstick for accurate measurements.

RINSING RICE
The most important thing to remember when rinsing the rice is to do it quickly. If rinsing is not done quickly, the rice will absorb the smell of the bran. This will ultimately cause the

MEASURING RICE

10

different types of rice

medium grain

long grain

long brown

arborio

short grain

short brown

RINSING RICE

ADDING WATER & MEASURING WATER (below)

cooked rice to have an unpleasant odor. First, add lots of water to the rice quickly, stir four to five times, and try to throw out the water in less than 10 seconds. Repeat several times until the water stops clouding. Rice may be washed right in Zojirushi rice cooker's inner cooking pan.

MUSENMAI—NO-RINSE RICE

Rinse-free rice (Musenmai) is a new type of rice that does not require rinsing. Rinse-free rice uses a different milling technique that eliminates the residues left on regular white rice. Due to this new milling technology, the grains of rinse-free rice are smoother and more slippery so more rinse-free rice fit in one cup than regular rice. When measured using a measuring cup, this variety will yield a three to five percent increase in the amount of rice. For this reason, it will be necessary to adjust the amount of the rice and/or water accordingly. You can use a rice measuring cup specifically made for Musenmai (which will adjust the amount of rice), or use the measuring line on the rice cooker pot specific for the Musenmai (which will adjust the amount of water) while using the standard rice measuring cup. You can also remove one heaping teaspoon of rice from the measuring cup and use the measuring line for regular white rice.

ADDING WATER

The rice cooker's inner cooking pan has measurement lines so that you only have to add water to the line marked inside the pan, without measuring. You should adjust the water level to your liking or to suit the type of rice you are cooking. There are several cookers now that allow you to choose between "softer" or "harder" cooked rice using the same amount of water.

SOAKING RICE

It is common to soak rice for 30 minutes in the summer and approximately two hours in the winter before cooking. Micom rice cookers are

PLACING INNER COOKING PAN

FLUFFING RICE

the exception because they have a preheat function that allows the heat to help the rice absorb water, making the soaking process unnecessary. You can now start the rice cooker immediately after rinsing. Also, in the timer cooking mode, the rice cooker will adjust the preheating time and begin cooking accordingly so that the rice will be done at the desired time.

FLUFFING RICE

As soon as the rice is cooked, fluff the rice to get rid of excess moisture. This prevents the rice from clumping together. Use a wooden spoon or the plastic spatula included with all rice cookers.

PRESERVING COOKED RICE

Rice can be kept warm in the rice cooker until served for up to 12 hours (or up to 20 hours in rice cookers with Extended Keep Warm mode). If you don't plan to eat the rice within 12 hours, here are some tips on how to keep the rice tasting fresh.

- Store in the fridge for up to five days in plastic containers.
- Store in the freezer for six to eight months in plastic freezer bags.

Leftover rice is also perfect for making fried rice because it's not as sticky as freshly cooked rice.

CLEANING THE RICE COOKER

If there is starch build-up on the inner lid or the steam vent, it may interfere with the rice-cooking process. Make sure to clean these areas often.

The inner cooking pan is lined with nonstick coating for easy cleaning. Please follow the instructions below to prolong the wear.

- Do not use metal utensils such as spoons and forks.

- Do not use the inner cooking pan as a washing tub.
- Do not use vinegar.
- When seasonings are used, wash the inner cooking pan as soon as possible.
- Do not use abrasive or harsh brushes or detergents.

ACCESSORIES

All Zojirushi rice cookers come with a rice measuring cup and nonstick rice spatula. These accessories are designed specifically for rice cookers to ensure the rice you cook turns out perfectly. The measuring cup measures about six ounces of rice. By using this measuring cup, you won't need to measure your water, as the lines inside your rice cooker indicate how much water to add. The nonstick rice spatula is supplied to prevent the inner cooking pan from being scratched by metal utensils and makes fluffing and serving rice easy. Wooden spatulas and spoons can also be used to prepare some of the recipes in this book.

Other accessories used for the recipes in this book include steaming baskets and ramekins. Both are available at your local supermarket or specialty kitchen store. Steaming baskets are usually available in stainless steel. When placing them inside the rice cooker, please be sure not to scratch the inner cooking pan. Ramekins are available in many sizes. We found that ramekins with about a $3\frac{1}{2}$ inch diameter work best with these recipes, although you can change their size as long as they fit in the rice cooker.

RICE COOKER CAPACITY

The rice cooker capacity is measured in how many cups of rice it can cook. A 10 cup rice cooker means it can cook 10 cups (rice measuring cup) of raw rice. The recipes listed in the following pages have been tested in various 10 cup rice cookers. When trying any of the recipes, follow the instructions for your rice cooker, and make sure the ingredients do not surpass the rice cooker's capacity and overflow.

white rice

4 **cups (rice measuring cup)**
   short grain white rice

MENU SETTING: **REGULAR**
SERVES **4**

1. Using the measuring cup that comes with the rice cooker, measure the rice accurately and put the rice in the inner cooking pan.

2. Add cold water to rinse the rice, and rub the rice with the palms of your hands. Rub gently so that you don't break the grain. Drain and repeat rinsing 3 to 4 times until the water becomes clear. This will result in fluffier and tastier rice.

3. Add water to the water level 4 marked inside the inner cooking pan. Distribute the rice evenly. All the rinsed rice should be submerged under the water.

4. Place the inner cooking pan in the rice cooker and push the Cook button. Make sure to wipe off any water outside the inner cooking pan.

5. When it turns to Keep Warm mode, leave the lid closed for about 15 more minutes. This will settle the rice. If you have a micom rice cooker, this will be done automatically.

6. Open the rice cooker, fluff the rice with a rice spatula to loosen the grains, and serve.

TIP

In China, Korea and Japan, where rice is served at almost every meal, the word for rice is synonymous with meal or food.

brown rice

MENU SETTING: BROWN RICE
SERVES 4

1. Using the measuring cup that comes with the rice cooker, measure the rice accurately and put the rice in the inner cooking pan.

2. Add cold water to rinse the rice, and rub the rice with the palms of your hands. Rub gently so that you don't break the grain. Drain and repeat rinsing 3 to 4 times until the water becomes clear. This will result in fluffier and tastier rice.

3. Add about 5 cups of water (or 1½ to 2 times the amount of water to rice) using the same measuring cup, or simply add water to the water level 3 of the Brown Rice setting marked inside the inner cooking pan (this works only if your rice cooker has the Brown Rice setting). Distribute the rice evenly. All the rinsed rice should be submerged under the water.

4. Make sure to wipe off any water outside the inner cooking pan. Place the inner cooking pan in the rice cooker, and choose Brown Rice setting (if your rice cooker has more than one setting). If your rice cooker does not have a Brown Rice setting, make sure to make the water adjustment above. Push the Cook button to start cooking.

5. When it turns to Keep Warm mode, leave the lid closed for about 15 more minutes. This will settle the rice. If you have a micom rice cooker, this will be done automatically.

6. Open the rice cooker, fluff the rice with a rice spatula to loosen the grains, and serve.

3 cups (rice measuring cup) brown rice

VARIATION
Try mixing wild rice (½ rice measuring cup) with brown rice (2½ rice measuring cup) for a healthy variation.

sushi rice

3   cups (rice measuring cup)
    short grain white rice

SUSHI VINEGAR:
4   tbs rice vinegar
3   tbs sugar
2   tsp salt

MENU SETTING: **SUSHI**
SERVES **4**

1. Using the measuring cup that comes with the rice cooker, measure the rice accurately and put the rice in the inner cooking pan.

2. Add cold water to rinse the rice, and rub the rice with the palms of your hands. Rub gently so that you don't break the grain. Drain and repeat rinsing 3 to 4 times until the water becomes clear. This will result in fluffier and tastier rice.

3. Add water to the water level 3 marked inside the inner cooking pan. Distribute the rice evenly. All the rinsed rice should be submerged under the water.

4. Place the inner cooking pan in the rice cooker, and choose the Sushi menu setting (this works only if your rice cooker has more than one setting). Make sure to wipe off any water outside the inner cooking pan. Push the Cook button to start cooking.

5. While cooking rice, prepare sushi vinegar by mixing rice vinegar, sugar, and salt in a small saucepan. Place the pan over low heat on the stovetop, allowing sugar to dissolve. Set aside to cool.

6. When the rice cooker turns to Keep Warm mode, leave the lid closed for about 15 more minutes. This will settle the rice. If you have a micom rice cooker, this will be done automatically.

7. Spread the rice into a large, 2-inch-deep plate (use a wooden bowl called sushi-oke if you have one), using a rice spatula.

8. Sprinkle cooled sushi vinegar over rice and fold rice with the rice spatula using quick motions, but never smash the rice.

9. To cool and remove the moisture from the rice, fan the rice as you mix it. Continue until the rice is cooled down to body temperature and looks glossy. Use immediately for rolls and sushi.

rice cooker creations

buttered rice

4	cups (rice measuring cup) long grain rice
4	cups (rice measuring cup) water or chicken stock
2	tbs unsalted butter
	Salt and pepper to taste

1. Using the measuring cup that comes with the rice cooker, measure the rice accurately and put the rice in the inner cooking pan.

2. Add cold water to rinse the rice, and rub the rice with the palms of your hands. Rub gently so that you don't break the rice grain. Drain the rice in a strainer and clean the inner cooking pan.

3. Place the empty inner cooking pan in the rice cooker. Push the Cook button of the rice cooker. Wait until the inner cooking pan is hot, and melt the butter.

4. Add the rice in the inner cooking pan and sauté for 3 to 4 minutes.

5. Pour in the water or stock. Adding the same amount of the liquid to the rice results in fluffier rice. Cover the lid and cook until it turns to Keep Warm mode. Add salt and pepper, and fluff the rice with the rice spatula.

6. Serve immediately.

VARIATION

This rice can also be cooled and used for the Rice Salad (see page 20 for recipe).

TIP

It is recommended to soak the rice for 30 minutes and place in the refrigerator before cooking. This presoaking is done automatically in micom rice cookers.

rice salad

2 cups cooked Buttered Rice
(see recipe on page 19)
¼ English (or hothouse)
cucumber, cubed
2 Roma tomatoes, seeded
and cubed
½ avocado, pitted, peeled,
and cubed
1 cup romaine salad mix
Salt and pepper to taste
1–2 tbs unsalted butter

MENU SETTING: **QUICK COOKING**
SERVES **4**

1. Cook the rice according to the Buttered Rice recipe.

2. Place the rice in a large mixing bowl to cool down.
Add the vegetables and mix well.

3. Add salt, pepper, and butter to taste.

TIP

The measuring cup that comes with your rice cooker is slightly smaller than your standard 8 ounce measuring cup. Why? In Japan, rice was measured in wooden boxes called Masu. It's the same little box Sake (Japanese rice wine) is served in. Because that was the standard measuring instrument for rice, the measuring cup that come with rice cookers were modeled after it. They are about 6 ounces in capacity.

rice cooker creations

tuna & avocado tower

2 cups Sushi Rice, cooked
(see recipe on page 18)
2 avocados, pitted, peeled,
and cut into $\frac{1}{2}$ -inch cubes
$\frac{1}{4}$ cup freshly squeezed
lemon juice
8 oz fresh sashimi quality
tuna, cut into $\frac{1}{2}$-inch cubes
4 white ramekins
($3\frac{1}{2}$ inch diameter)
Salad or sprouts as garnish
(optional)

VARIATION

For color variation, try switching the layers of avocados with that of tuna so that the tuna layer comes on top.

MENU SETTING: SUSHI / REGULAR
SERVES 4

1. Prepare rice as directed in the Sushi Rice recipe.

2. Wet the inside of the ramekins with a little bit of water.

3. Spread $\frac{1}{4}$ of the avocados in an even layer on the bottom of the ramekins.

4. Over avocado, spread about 2 ounces of cubed tuna and top with $\frac{1}{2}$ cup of sushi rice, spreading each in an even layer. Push the rice down to add as much sushi rice as possible.

5. Repeat steps 3 and 4 for all the ramekins.

6. Turn the ramekin upside down into a plate, so the rice layer is on the bottom. Serve garnished with salad or sprouts.

TIP

Rice is also beneficial for beauty! Rice is healthy and can benefit diets, but the bran is also very good for your skin. Rice bran is rich in oil, makes an effective exfoliant, and contains phytic acid, a B-complex vitamin that can help improve blood circulation and stimulate cell turnover when used topically.

spanish rice

MENU SETTING: QUICK COOKING
SERVES 4

1. Soak the rice in a bowl of hot water for about 10 minutes. Strain and rinse under cold running water. Drain and set aside.

2. Push the Cook button of the rice cooker and add oil, onion, garlic, fresh and canned tomatoes with juice in the inner cooking pan and cook for about 5 to 7 minutes.

3. Stir in the reserved drained rice and chicken stock and mix well. Season to taste with salt and pepper, and close the lid.

4. When rice cooker turns to Keep Warm mode, stir in the peas and leave the lid closed for another 5 minutes.

5. Spoon the rice in serving dish and garnish with cilantro.

TIP

Rice bran is a natural make-up ingredient that also protects against damage from harmful ultra-violet rays. More and more cosmetics, lotions, and shampoos made from rice bran are showing up in stores.

$2\frac{1}{2}$ cups (rice measuring cup) long grain rice
2 tbs extra virgin olive oil
$\frac{1}{2}$ medium onion, finely chopped
1-2 cloves garlic, finely chopped
2 fresh tomatoes, peeled and finely chopped
1 cup chopped, canned tomato with juice (about $\frac{1}{2}$ cup)
$1\frac{1}{2}$ cups chicken stock (use can or see recipe on page 45)
Salt and pepper to taste
1 cup fresh or frozen peas
Few sprigs fresh cilantro for garnish

saffron risotto with herbed scampi

SERVES **4**

1. Marinate the shrimps with Italian blend herbs, olive oil, salt, and pepper in a container. Cover and leave it in the refrigerator for 10 to 20 minutes.

2. Push the Cook button of the rice cooker to heat the inner cooking pan and melt half of the butter. Add the chopped onion and cook for about 5 minutes covered.

3. Pour the white wine and wait about 4 to 5 minutes uncovered, until alcohol smell goes away. Add the rice and stir well to coat the grains with the butter. Add 1 cup of the chicken stock and cook, stirring until almost all the liquid has evaporated.

4. Add the saffron to 1 cup of the hot stock in another pot, stirring until the color of the soup changes to yellowish red. Add a ladleful of the stock to the inner cooking pan at a time, cover the lid, stirring occasionally (2 to 3 times). Repeat the procedure as the rice absorbs the stock.

5. Continue adding remaining 4 cups of the stock, until the rice is creamy, but the grains are still firm.

6. Stir in remaining butter, and add the marinated shrimps.

7. Cover the lid and cook the risotto for a few more minutes before serving. Season to taste with salt and pepper.

8. Serve with Parmesan cheese on top.

½   cup unsalted butter
½   onion, finely chopped
1   cup white wine
2½ cups (rice measuring cup) Arborio rice
2   cups hot chicken stock (use can or see recipe on page 45)
4   cups vegetable stock (use can or see recipe on page 44)
1   pinch saffron
¼   cup freshly grated Parmesan cheese
Salt and pepper to taste

MARINADE:
1   tsp Italian blend herbs
2   tsp extra virgin olive oil
Salt and pepper to taste
12 shrimps (21–25 cts or about ½ lb), peeled and deveined

confetti couscous salad

½ cups vegetable or chicken stock (use can or see recipe on pages 44–45)
1 cup couscous

CONFETTI HERBED OIL:
3 tbs extra olive oil
5 kalamata olives, halved
3 oz feta cheese, crumbled
1 tbs fresh lemon juice
2 sprigs fresh oregano leaves, finely chopped
2 tbs red bell pepper, finely chopped
Salt and pepper to taste

MENU SETTING: QUICK COOKING
SERVES 4

1. Pour the stock into the inner cooking pan. Set the steaming basket inside and place in the rice cooker.

2. Push the Cook button and bring the stock to a boil (about 10 minutes).

3. While boiling the stock, rinse the couscous in cold water. Drain.

4. Line the steaming basket with greaseproof paper and spoon the couscous in.

5. Close the lid and steam the couscous for 5 minutes or longer until the couscous is fluffy when separated with fork. Turn off the rice cooker, and set the couscous aside to cool.

6. In a medium bowl, combine all confetti herbed oil ingredients and set aside.

7. When couscous is cooled down, stir in confetti herbed oil mixture, add salt and pepper, and serve.

TIP

Store-bought rice and other commercial grain mixes cook up perfectly in your rice cooker. Or, make your own savory rice using stocks with spices instead of plain water.

oatmeal porridge

MENU SETTING: QUICK COOKING
SERVES 4

1. Place the rolled oats, water, salt, honey (or maple syrup), and ground cinnamon in the inner cooking pan and place in the rice cooker. Close the lid and push the Cook button.

2. After it begins to boil (about 10 minutes), stir every 5 minutes, and check if the liquid has been absorbed.

3. Pour into bowls hot, and top with a splash of heavy cream or half & half.

1   cup rolled oats
3   cups water
¼   tsp salt
1   tbs honey or pure maple syrup (or to taste)
Pinch ground cinnamon
¼   cup heavy cream or half & half

TIP

Lots of stovetop dishes, such as steel-cut oats and Southern-style grits, are much easier to prepare and cook in the rice cooker.

stuffed bell pepper with couscous

2   green bell peppers,
     halved lengthwise or
     in top and bottom
1½   cups vegetable or chicken
     stock (use can or see recipe
     on pages 44–45)
1   cup couscous
2   tbs extra virgin olive oil
¼   medium onion,
     finely chopped
1   medium carrot, peeled
     and diced in little cubes
½   red bell pepper, diced
     in little cubes
Salt and pepper to taste

VARIATION
Try with bell peppers
with other colors (e.g.
orange, yellow, red)

MENU SETTING: **QUICK COOKING**
SERVES **4**

1. Pour 1 cup of water in the inner cooking pan of the rice cooker. Set a steaming basket inside and place in the rice cooker.

2. Arrange the bell peppers with the skin side down in the steam basket and push the Cook button. Cook for 10 minutes.

3. Turn off the rice cooker and take the green bell peppers out of the rice cooker. Clean the inner cooking pan well.

4. Pour chicken stock to the inner cooking pan and push the Cook button to bring to a boil (about 10 minutes). If the rice cooker does not turn on, allow to cool, then try again. Stir in the couscous, cover the lid, and turn off the rice cooker immediately. Let stand until tender, about 5 minutes.

5. Season with salt and pepper. Fluff the couscous with a spatula and set aside. Clean the inner cooking pan well.

6. Push the Cook button and start the rice cooker to heat the inner cooking pan. Pour the olive oil and sauté the onions, carrots, and red bell pepper with spatula until tender, but still firm. Turn off the rice cooker.

7. Mix the couscous and the vegetables in the inner cooking pan, and adjust with salt and pepper.

8. Stuff the mixture into the green bell peppers. Wash the inner cooking pan.

9. Pour 1 cup of water in the inner cooking pan, set the steaming basket inside and place in the rice cooker. Put the stuffed bell peppers on the steaming basket, push the Cook button and close the lid to steam for 10 more minutes.

10. Serve immediately as a side dish.

moroccan chicken & vegetable couscous

CHICKEN:

2	onions, roughly chopped
2	tbs olive oil
2	pieces skinless chicken breasts, cut into halves
2	cloves garlic, crushed
½	tbs salt or to taste
1	tsp ground fresh pepper or to taste
½	tsp ground cinnamon
¼	tsp ground ginger
¼	tsp ground turmeric
¼	tsp ground cumin
½	lb carrots, peeled and diced 3- x 1-inch
½	lb turnip or daikon, peeled and cut into 3- x 1-inch
½	lb pumpkin or squash, peeled and cut into 3- x 1-inch (optional)
10	stems fresh parsley, with leaves
10	stems fresh cilantro and leaves
½	lb zucchini, cut into 3- x 1-inch
1	large tomato, chopped (or 1 can diced tomato, about 28 oz)
½	can chickpeas, drained (about 15 oz)
½	green bell pepper, cut in ½-inch strips (optional)
1	tbs tomato paste (to thicken; optional)
	Harissa to taste (Moroccan Chili paste; optional)

MENU SETTING: QUICK COOKING
SERVES 4

1. To prepare the chicken: push the Cook button of the rice cooker and heat the inner cooking pan. Sauté the onions with the olive oil until soft.

2. Add the chicken and brown both sides until golden brown. If the meat does not brown, just sauté until the color changes on both sides.

3. Add garlic, salt, pepper and remaining spices, and cook for another 5 minutes.

4. Add water, just enough to cover the chicken (be sure not to pour the water directly on the chicken as this will make the chicken tough), and simmer for 5 to 10 minutes.

5. Add carrots, turnips (or daikon), and pumpkin (optional). Add stems of parsley and cilantro. Cook for about 20 minutes or until the vegetables are slightly cooked.

6. Add zucchini, tomato, chickpeas, and green bell pepper (optional) and cook for another 20 minutes, or until the vegetables are cooked, but still firm.

7. If the chickens are fully cooked, remove them and cover to keep warm for 10 more minutes until the vegetables are soft.

8. To prepare the couscous: mix couscous with salt and water in a bowl. Leave to soak for 5 minutes and drain. Add the raisins or sultanas, and nutmeg to the couscous if desired.

9. Place couscous in a flat container with some depth, add half cup of hot water, and heat in the microwave for 1 minute on high setting. Cover the container and leave for 15 minutes (also see Confetti Couscous Salad on page 26 on how to prepare the couscous in the rice cooker).

10. Fluff the couscous with rice spatula and taste to see if it is ready. It should be fluffy, almost bouncy. One method for testing is to take one grain and place in between your index finger and thumb and smash it! If it becomes a paste, then it is ready.

11. When both the vegetables and couscous are cooked, bring back the chicken to the inner cooking pan. If the broth is too runny, add the tomato paste and cook for an additional 3 to 4 minutes, until the desired consistency.

COUSCOUS:
1½ **cups couscous**
1 **cup water or as directed in the packet**
1 **tsp salt**
2 **tbs raisins or sultanas (optional)**
Pinch fresh nutmeg, grated (optional)

TIP

1. Pour the couscous evenly on a large flat platter and make an indentation or well in the middle. Place the chicken pieces in the well.

2. Using a slotted spoon, begin removing the vegetables from the liquid in the pot and pile them up on the chicken; the vegetables should be used to form a cone on top of and around the meat. You may need to place the vegetables by hand in order for them to stay in place.

3. Strain the liquid from the pot and gently pour about 2 cups of it over the vegetables and the couscous. Be careful not to wash the vegetables down the side of the cone.

4. Pour the remaining broth in a bowl and put on the table for the guests to serve. To spice up the broth, dissolve 2 to 3 tablespoons of Harissa in the broth if desired.

cannellini beans, cabbage & beef stew

MENU SETTING: QUICK COOKING
SERVES 4

1. Soak the beans in warm water overnight in the refrigerator. Change water at least once. Drain and set aside. Skip this step if using canned beans.

2. Push the Cook button and heat the inner cooking pan for 5 minutes. Pour olive oil, onion, fennel, and garlic to sauté for 1 to 2 minutes.

3. Add the beef cubes in batches and sauté until all the sides are slightly brown.

4. Gradually add crushed tomato, beans, and 3 cups of water and cover the lid.

5. When it turns to Keep Warm mode, add the strips of cabbage.

6. Leave it in Keep Warm mode for about 30 minutes or until beef is falling apart. Salt to taste.

½ lb dry cannellini beans, soaked in water overnight (or use can, 15–16 oz)
4 tbs extra virgin olive oil
½ onion, chopped
1 branch fennel, coarsely chopped
2 cloves garlic, finely chopped
1 lb beef stew meat, cut into 1½-inch cubes
1 can tomato, peeled and crushed (15-16 oz)
1 lb cabbage, roughly cut into 1-inch strips
Salt to taste

GRAIN

chickpea & bell pepper salad

¾ lb dry chickpeas, soaked
   in water overnight
4 cups water
⅓ red bell pepper,
   cut into ¼-inch strips
⅓ yellow bell pepper,
   cut into ¼-inch strips
⅓ green bell pepper,
   cut into ¼-inch strips
1 can water-packed tuna
   (about 6–7 oz)
2 tbs capers, drained
2-3 basil leaves, torn into
   rough pieces

DRESSING:
1 tsp garlic, finely chopped
2 tbs red wine vinegar
3 tbs extra virgin olive oil
Salt and pepper to taste

MENU SETTING: **QUICK COOKING**
SERVES **4**

1. Soak the chickpeas in water overnight in the refrigerator. Change the water at least once.

2. Drain the chickpeas, transfer to the inner cooking pan with 4 cups of water, close the lid, and push the Cook button of the rice cooker.

3. When the rice cooker turns to Keep Warm mode and chickpeas are soft, drain the peas, let them cool, and set aside.

4. Open the tuna can, drain, and set aside.

5. To prepare dressing: in a mixing bowl, add garlic, red wine vinegar, olive oil, salt, and pepper and mix.

6. In a separate serving dish, mix the reserved chickpeas, bell peppers, capers, and tuna.

7. Drizzle the dressing over the chickpea salad. Serve with basil leaves over top.

basic pasta cooking

8   cups water (2 quarts)
1   tbs salt
2   tbs extra virgin olive oil
1   lb dry pasta
1   cup cold water

Any kind of sauce (or see
    Marinara Sauce recipe
    on page 40)

VARIATIONS

**Prepare sauce, add the pasta
and mix well.**

**For hot dish, add 1 tablespoon
of olive oil in the inner cooking
pan and place in rice cooker.
Push the Cook button and add
the sauce and the pasta. Mix
until pasta is well coated with
the sauce and hot. Serve
immediately.**

**For a cold pasta salad, mix all
ingredients together and keep
in refrigerator until ready to
serve.**

MENU SETTING: QUICK COOKING
SERVES 4

1. Fill the inner cooking pan with water and place in the rice cooker. Add salt and push the Cook button to start cooking.

2. When water boils (10 to 15 minutes), add 1 tablespoon of olive oil and the pasta.

3. While cooking, stir the pasta with wooden spoon so the pasta does not stick together. If the pasta absorbs all the water, add 1 cup of cold water.

4. Cook the pasta until al dente ("when it is right for the tooth" in Italian), which means soft but firm, and never overcooked.

5. Drain the pasta in a colander. Rinse well under cold water. Coat the pasta with remaining olive oil and reserve. Serve with your favorite pasta sauce or Marinara Sauce recipe.

egg salad

1. Put the eggs in the inner cooking pan with enough water to cover the eggs. Cover the lid, push the Cook button, and cook for 18 to 20 minutes.

2. Peel and chop the eggs and set aside.

3. Add the remaining ingredients in a medium bowl and mix.

4. Add the reserved eggs and mix thoroughly, without smashing the eggs.

5. Serve as a salad or for sandwich filling.

7–8 eggs
2   tbs finely chopped onion
2   tbs finely chopped celery
1   tbs pickle relish, squeezed
    out of excess liquid
½   tsp celery seeds
4   tbs mayonnaise
1   tbs Dijon mustard
Salt to taste
2   tbs finely chopped
    fresh parsley

NON-GRAIN

pasta salad
with mushrooms

1. Cook pasta in the rice cooker (refer to the Basic Pasta Cooking recipe on page 36).

2. Rinse pasta under cold water, drain well, and coat with olive oil. Set aside.

3. To prepare the balsamic dressing: combine all the ingredients in a bowl and set aside.

4. Place the pasta and feta cheese with all the vegetables in a serving bowl and mix well. Blend with reserved dressing and serve.

8   oz pasta (e.g., penne, fusilli, bowtie)
2   tbs olive oil, to coat the cooked and rinsed pasta
6   oz button mushrooms, sliced
¼   small red onion, cut into thin strips
⅓   green or yellow bell pepper, cut into thin strips
10–12 black olives, halved and seeded
1   Roma tomato, seeded and cut into thin strips
2   oz feta cheese, crumbled

BALSAMIC DRESSING:
3   tbs extra virgin olive oil
1   tbs balsamic vinegar
2   tsp honey
1   clove garlic, minced
2   tsp chopped fresh Italian blend herbs (or dried)
1   tbs chopped fresh basil

NON-GRAIN

marinara sauce

3   oz olive oil (about $\frac{1}{3}$ cup)
1   cup onion, chopped
1   stalk celery, chopped
2   cloves garlic, minced
$\frac{2}{3}$ cup chicken stock
     (use can or see recipe
     on page 45)
1   bouquet garni (fresh basil,
     thyme, bay leaf, and
     oregano)
2   cups plum tomatoes,
     seeded and chopped
2   cups diced tomatoes,
     canned with juice
2   tbs sugar
Salt and pepper to taste

MENU SETTING: **QUICK COOKING**
SERVES **4**

1. Push the Cook button of the rice cooker and heat olive oil in the inner cooking pan. Add onion, celery, and garlic.

2. Sauté until softened. Stir in plum tomatoes, diced tomatoes, and sugar.

3. Add chicken stock and bouquet garni. Close the lid, bring to boil and simmer (about 10 to15 minutes). If less runny sauce is preferred, cook until the rice cooker turns to Keep Warm mode.

4. Adjust with seasoning, discard bouquet garni, and serve with pasta or other main dish.

fettuccine alfredo

1. Push the Cook button of the rice cooker to warm up the inner cooking pan. Melt 4 tablespoons of butter in the inner cooking pan.

2. Add cheese, cream, remaining butter, salt and pepper, combine well, and bring to a boil.

3. Stir in cooked fettuccine and toss to coat.

4. Serve the pasta sprinkled with parsley and cheese.

12	oz fettuccine, cooked al dente (see Basic Pasta Cooking recipe on page 36)
6	tbs unsalted butter, cubed
½	cup freshly grated Parmesan cheese
⅔	cup heavy cream

Salt and pepper to taste
Fresh Italian parsley, finely chopped for garnish
Fresh Parmesan cheese, grated for garnish

VARIATION
Add cooked chicken, shrimp, or favorite vegetables to pasta.

NON-GRAIN

orzo pasta with ham, peas & sun-dried tomatoes

8   cups water
1   lb orzo (small pasta shaped
     like barley)
4   tbs extra virgin olive oil
2   tsp salt
Fresh parsley, chopped for
     garnish

CREAM SAUCE:
1   cup heavy cream
2   cloves garlic, minced
¼   cup diced ham
¼   cup peas
4–5 sun-dried tomatoes
2   tbs freshly grated
     Parmesan cheese
2   tbs chopped fresh parsley

MENU SETTING: **QUICK COOKING**
SERVES **4**

1. Pour the water in the inner cooking pan, close the lid, and push the Cook button. Bring to boil (about 10 minutes), add orzo, 2 tablespoons olive oil, and salt. Cook for about 8 minutes, stirring occasionally. Turn off the rice cooker.

2. Strain the orzo pasta, rinse with cold water, coat with remaining 2 tablespoons of olive oil and set aside. Clean the inner cooking pan.

3. To prepare the cream sauce: add the heavy cream and garlic in the inner cooking pan, push the Cook button, cover for about 10 minutes, or until the cream boils, and add the remaining ingredients.

4. Add the reserved orzo pasta. Cover and cook for 3 to 5 minutes.

5. Sprinkle with more parsley for garnish and serve immediately.

basic vegetable stock

½   small onion, roughly cubed
1   sprig celery, chopped
1   small carrot, peeled
    and cubed
1   bay leaf
8–10 black Peppercorn
4–8 stems fresh parsley
5   cups water

MENU SETTING: QUICK COOKING
SERVES 4

1. Wash and prepare the vegetables.

2. Place the prepared vegetables, bay leaf, black peppercorn, parsley stems, and water in the inner cooking pan.

3. Place the inner cooking pan in the rice cooker, close the lid, and push the Cook button to start cooking.

4. After the rice cooker turns to Keep Warm mode, wait for an additional 10 to 15 minutes, without opening the lid.

5. Remove the stock from the inner cooking pan and strain the vegetables and the bay leaf.

6. Use stock immediately or refrigerate in tight container for one day.

rice cooker creations

basic chicken stock

1. Cut the chicken into pieces. Wash under running cold water and pat dry with paper towel. Reserve.

2. Fill the inner cooking pan with cold water, place the reserved chicken pieces inside, and place in the rice cooker. Close the lid and push the Cook button.

3. In a cheesecloth, place the bay leaves, thyme, peppercorns and parsley stems and tie with a cotton string to make bouquet garni.

4. When the stock starts to boil (10 to 15 minutes), skim the scum off top carefully.

5. Add the cheesecloth and the chopped vegetables in the inner cooking pan. Add water if necessary to keep bones covered. Close the lid.

6. When the rice cooker turns to Keep Warm mode, leave it in Keep Warm mode for another 20 minutes without opening the lid.

7. Strain the content of the inner cooking pan through a strainer lined with layer of cheesecloth.

8. Cool the stock, vented in ice cold water bath. Place in refrigerator overnight.

9. Remove solidified fat from surface of liquid and store in a container with a lid in the refrigerator for 2 to 3 days, or in the freezer for up to 3 months. Defrost in the refrigerator and bring to a boil for 2 minutes before using.

10. Use as a base for soups and sauces.

$\frac{1}{2}$ **fresh chicken with skin and bones (about 1$\frac{1}{2}$ lb)**
10 **cups cold water**
1 **bouquet garni (bay leaves, thyme, peppercorns, parsley stem)**
1 **onion, chopped**
$\frac{1}{2}$ **carrot, chopped**
1-2 **stalks celery, chopped**

NON-GRAIN

minestrone

1. Push the Cook button and wait until the inner cooking pan is hot (about 3 to 5 minutes). Heat olive oil, add onions, celery, and carrots, and mix. Add garlic and heat for about 5 minutes, or well sweat. Add chicken stock. Cover the lid and bring it to boil, about 10 to 15 minutes.

2. When the stock begins to boil, stir in zucchini, kidney beans, green beans, pasta, tomatoes, corn, and cooked chicken breast, if using.

3. Add the herbs and season with salt and pepper. Cover the lid and cook for another 5 minutes.

4. Serve hot with toasted garlic bread for light lunch or as a first course.

2	tbs olive oil
$\frac{1}{2}$	cup onions, chopped
1	stalk celery, sliced
$\frac{1}{4}$	cup carrots, diced
2	cloves garlic, minced
10	cups chicken stock (use can or see recipe on page 45)
2	tbs zucchini, diced
$\frac{1}{4}$	cup kidney beans, cooked or canned
2	tbs green beans, cut into $1\frac{1}{2}$ inch strip
$\frac{1}{2}$	cup cooked pasta (e.g., penne, bowties, ziti; see recipe on page 36)
$\frac{1}{2}$	cup Roma tomatoes (about 2 tomatoes), peeled, seeded and chopped
$\frac{1}{4}$	cup corn, fresh or frozen (optional)
1	cup cooked chicken breast strips (optional)
2	tbs chopped fresh Italian blend herbs (or dried)
Salt and pepper to taste	

NON-GRAIN

tomato soup

2   oz potatoes, peeled
    and diced
2   lb ripe tomatoes,
    peeled, cut into quarters
    and seeded
¼   onion, roughly chopped
    in ¾-inch cubes
2   tbs unsalted butter
4   cups vegetable stock
    (use can or see recipe
    on page 44)
1   tbs finely chopped
    Italian parsley
Salt to taste
Pinch sugar
4 dollops crème fraîche

VARIATIONS
Blanch tomatoes, peel, and
seed. Chop into ¼-inch cubes
and garnish with parsley and
crème fraîche.

Serve soup with garlic butter
croutons (can be store bought).

Serve as light lunch with
salad and toast or as first
course for dinner.

MENU SETTING: **QUICK COOKING**
SERVES **4**

1. Place the tomatoes, onion, and potatoes in the inner cooking
   pan. Add butter and vegetable stock and place in rice cooker.
   Push the Cook button.

2. When the rice cooker turns to Keep Warm mode, remove the
   soup from the inner cooking pan, purée, and season with salt
   and sugar.

3. Ladle the soup into soup bowls, and add a dollop of crème
   fraîche on top. Sprinkle the Italian parsley.

chicken noodle soup

MENU SETTING: QUICK COOKING
SERVES 4–6

1. Push the Cook button of the rice cooker to heat the inner cooking pan. Pour the olive oil and sauté the garlic, shallots, mushrooms, and shiitake mushrooms (optional).

2. Add the white wine, and let it evaporate, about 2 minutes, or until the alcohol smell goes away. Add the chicken stock, chicken breast pieces, thyme, and cooked pasta. Cover and cook for 10 to 15 minutes, or until the soup is hot.

3. Season with salt and pepper. Garnish with parsley. Serve immediately.

2	tsp olive oil
2	cloves garlic, finely minced (or 1 tsp minced garlic)
2	shallots, finely chopped
½	cup sliced button mushroom
3–4	dried shiitake mushroom, soaked, drained, and sliced (optional)
1	cup white wine
4–6	cups chicken stock (use can or see recipe on page 45)
8	oz chicken breast pieces, poached in hot chicken stock for 5–10 minutes (or use frozen cooked chicken breast)
2	tsp chopped fresh thyme
1	cup cooked pasta (e.g., bowtie, farfalle, orzo, orechiette; see recipe on page 36)
Salt and pepper to taste	
½	cup chopped fresh parsley for garnish

NON-GRAIN

salmon with vegetables

4   salmon fillets (about
    4 oz each)
1   lemon, cut into slices
2   sprigs fresh dill or oregano
4   tbs olive oil
Salt and pepper to taste
1   carrot, peeled and cut into
    thin strips (julienne)
½   red or green bell
    pepper, cut into thin
    strips (julienne)
½   red onion, cut into thin
    strips (julienne)
⅛   fennel bulb, cut into thin
    strips (julienne)
2   tbs unsalted butter

MENU SETTING: **QUICK COOKING**
SERVES **4**

1. Place the salmon fillets in a flat glass container, add the lemon slices, herbs, and 2 tablespoons of olive oil. Add salt and pepper to taste. Cover with plastic wrap and refrigerate for 1 to 2 hours.

2. Push the Cook button of the rice cooker and warm up the inner cooking pan. Add remaining 2 tablespoons of olive oil. Wait until the inner cooking pan is hot (about 3 to 5 minutes), add all the vegetables and sauté until soft, but crispy. Turn off the rice cooker.

3. Cut 4 pieces of parchment paper, each measuring 6 X 8 inches. Divide the vegetables and the butter into 4 equal parts and place in the papers. Clean the inner cooking pan.

4. Take the salmon fillets and place them on top of the vegetables. Season with salt and pepper, if needed. Fold the parchment papers to seal.

5. Add 1 cup of water in the inner cooking pan, and set the steaming basket inside. Place the parchment papers on top of the steaming basket. Push the Cook button. Cover and cook for 20 minutes. If the parchment papers are stacked, switch the top parchment with bottom ones and cook for another 10 minutes.

6. Take out the parchment papers from the rice cooker to serving plates, cut the parchment paper with scissors to show the salmon fillets in the pocket. Serve with rice or by itself.

smoked salmon gratin

3 tsp olive oil or spray
8 oz smoked salmon fillets, cut into thumb-size bite cubes
½ red onion, sliced
1 clove garlic, finely minced
2–3 sprigs fresh dill, chopped
1½ cups heavy cream
3 oz lemon juice
Salt and pepper to taste
4 tsp grated Swiss cheese

MENU SETTING: QUICK COOKING
SERVES **4**

1. With 1½ teaspoons of the oil, lightly grease 4 ramekins (3½-inch diameter).

2. Push the Cook button and add the remaining 1½ teaspoons of the oil to the inner cooking pan. Wait until the pan is hot (about 3 to 5 minutes) and sauté the red onion until soft (4 to 5 minutes). Stir in the garlic and sauté for 1 minute.

3. Divide the onion mixture and cubed smoked salmon in the ramekins. Clean the inner cooking pan well.

4. In a bowl, mix the dill, heavy cream, lemon juice, salt, and pepper. Divide cream sauce equally into the ramekins.

5. Top each ramekin with cheese and place in the inner cooking pan. Place the inner cooking pan in the rice cooker. Put two ramekins at a time if all four do not fit in the rice cooker.

6. Push the Cook button. Once the rice cooker turns to Keep Warm mode, leave it in Keep Warm for another 10 minutes. Take the ramekins out of the inner cooking pan, and let it settle for 15 minutes.

7. Place under a grill for a few minutes to brown the cheese. Serve as appetizer or side dish.

beef stew

1. In a small bowl, add salt, pepper, and wine. Pour over beef chuck, cover, and marinate for 30 minutes in the refrigerator.

2. Take out the beef and pat dry with paper towel, then dredge into flour. Discard excess flour.

3. Push the Cook button of the rice cooker, heat the inner cooking pan and stir in butter and grapeseed oil until butter is melted.

4. Sauté the garlic slightly, then sauté the beef cubes until all the sides are slightly brown.

5. Add tomato juice. Cover to bring to boil, stirring constantly with a spatula, to scrape any brown bits from the pan.

6. Add beef stock and bouquet garni and bring to a boil.

7. Add pearl onions, baby carrots, and parsnips. Cover and simmer. When it turns to Keep Warm mode, leave it in Keep Warm mode and stir occasionally for 20 minutes or longer, until the beef becomes tender.

8. Discard the bouquet garni and add peas.

9. Cover and leave for another 3 minutes or until the peas are warm and cooked. Add salt and pepper to taste.

10. Pour in a platter and sprinkle with parsley. Serve immediately with pasta or rice.

Salt and pepper to taste
$\frac{1}{2}$ cup red wine
$1\frac{1}{2}$ lb boneless beef chuck, cubed into $1\frac{1}{2}$-inch cubes
1 tbs unsalted butter
2 tbs grapeseed oil
2 tbs all-purpose flour
1 clove garlic, minced
$\frac{2}{3}$ cup tomato juice
$2\frac{1}{3}$ cups beef stock
1 bouquet garni (thyme, parsley, bay leaf)
7–8 pearl onions, peeled
7–8 baby carrots, peeled
2 medium parsnips, peeled and cut into $1\frac{1}{2}$-inch cubes
$\frac{1}{2}$ cup frozen peas
Fresh parsley, chopped for garnish

NON-GRAIN

ossobucco

MENU SETTING: **QUICK COOKING**
SERVES 8–10

1. Pat veal shanks dry and sprinkle with salt and pepper.

2. Sprinkle with flour and shake off excess flour.

3. Push the Cook button of the rice cooker. Add olive oil and heat in the inner cooking pan.

4. Place the shanks in the inner cooking pan and brown in batches. Reserve in a warm plate.

5. Drain the fat from the inner cooking pan. Add red wine and leave the rice cooker uncovered until the wine evaporates (about 3 to 5 minutes). Pour off the remaining wine into reserved meat. Turn off the rice cooker and clean the inner cooking pan.

6. Make bouquet garni (tie bay leaf, parsley, and thyme sprigs) and set aside.

7. Push the Cook button of the rice cooker and melt the butter in the inner cooking pan. If the rice cooker does not turn on, allow to cool, and then try again. Sauté the carrots, onion, celery, and garlic. Cook until softened.

8. Bring back the reserved meat and add bouquet garni, tomatoes, and tomato paste. Salt and pepper to taste.

9. Add the stock. Cover and continue to cook. When the rice cooker turns to Keep Warm mode, leave it for another 1 hour in Keep Warm mode, or until the meat can be pulled away from the bone and is tender.

10. To prepare the gremolata: mix all ingredients together and sprinkle over the ossobuco when serving.

4	veal shanks (5–6 oz each), 4 inches in diameter and no more than 2 inches thick
1	tsp salt
½	tsp pepper
2	tbs all-purpose flour
2	tbs olive oil
¾	cup dry red wine
1	bay leaf
3	sprigs fresh parsley
2	sprigs fresh thyme
2	tbs unsalted butter
1	medium carrot, peeled and finely chopped
½	medium onion, finely chopped
1	rib celery, finely chopped
1	clove large garlic, minced
2	plum tomatoes, seeded and chopped
2	tsp tomato paste
	Salt and pepper to taste
4	cups veal or beef stock

GREMOLATA:

4	tbs finely chopped fresh parsley
1½	tbs finely grated lemon zest
1	tsp minced garlic

NON-GRAIN

stuffed eggplant with tomato sauce & cheese

TOMATO SAUCE:

1	tbs olive oil
¼	onion, finely chopped
3	cloves garlic, finely chopped
8	oz peeled, whole tomatoes, canned
1	tbs Italian blend herbs

EGGPLANT:

2	small eggplants, halved lengthwise
¼	cup water
½	cup grated cheese

MENU SETTING: QUICK COOKING
SERVES 4

1. To prepare the tomato sauce: push the Cook button and pour olive oil into the inner cooking pan to heat. When it is hot, add the onion and garlic, stir quickly, let soften a bit.

2. Add tomatoes and Italian blend herbs. Crush the tomatoes into chunks. Close the lid and simmer.

3. When the rice cooker turns to Keep Warm mode, pour the content into a container, setting aside. Turn off the rice cooker and clean the inner cooking pan.

4. Pour water into the inner cooking pan, place a steaming basket inside.

5. Put the eggplant halves on the steaming basket with the skin side down. Stack or put two pieces at a time if all four do not fit on the steaming basket. Cover the lid and push the Cook button. If the rice cooker does not turn on, allow to cool, and then try again. Steam for 12 to 15 minutes or until the eggplants become soft. Take out the eggplants and turn off the rice cooker.

6. Cool the eggplant, scoop out the flesh without breaking the skin, and stuff with reserved tomato sauce.

7. Top the eggplants with grated cheese and place them back on the steaming basket in the inner cooking pan. Push the Cook button again and cook for 5 to 7 minutes. Put two pieces at a time if all four do not fit.

8. Serve immediately.

mashed potatoes with parmesan cheese

2   lbs Yukon gold potatoes,
    peeled and cut into 4 parts
¼   cup heavy cream or
    half & half
⅔   cup milk
¼   cup butter
Pinch nutmeg
Salt and pepper to taste
Freshly grated Parmesan
    cheese for garnish

MENU SETTING: **QUICK COOKING**
SERVES **4**

1. Place the potatoes in the inner cooking pan with a little bit of salt and water just enough to cover the potatoes.

2. Place the inner cooking pan in the rice cooker, close the lid, push the Cook button, and cook until the potatoes become soft.

3. Transfer the potatoes to a bowl and mash the potatoes. While the potatoes are still warm, mix in the heavy cream, milk, butter, nutmeg, salt, and pepper.

4. Before serving, top the potatoes with cheese.

stuffed potatoes with three cheeses

MENU SETTING: QUICK COOKING
SERVES 4

2	large potatoes, halved
2	tbs unsalted butter, at room temperature
2	tbs milk
2	tbs heavy cream
Salt and pepper to taste	
1	cup grated cheese (combination of cheddar, Parmesan, and Monterey Jack)
4	tbs chopped fresh parsley

1. Place the potato halves in the inner cooking pan with ⅔ cup of water, place in the rice cooker and push the Cook button.

2. Insert a skewer in the middle of the potatoes to test if they are tender. When the potatoes are cooked, remove from the inner cooking pan and turn off the rice cooker. Clean the inner cooking pan.

3. Cool slightly and empty the cooked potatoes with spoon without breaking the skin.

4. Mash the potatoes in a bowl, add butter, milk, cream, salt and pepper, and mix well.

5. Fill the potato skins with the mashed potato mixture.

6. Place the filled potatoes in the inner cooking pan and sprinkle with cheese. Place the inner cooking pan in the rice cooker.

7. Push the Cook button. If the rice cooker does not turn on, allow to cool, and then try again. Cook the potatoes until cheese is melted.

8. Sprinkle the chopped parsley and serve immediately.

steamed artichokes with lemon butter sauce

MENU SETTING: QUICK COOKING
SERVES 4

1. Grate the lemon and squeeze out the juice into a small bowl.

2. Clean the artichokes by removing the stems, the spines, and the hard outer leaves. Remove the chokes and sprinkle with lemon juice.

3. Place the artichokes in the inner cooking pan, and drizzle with olive oil and white wine.

4. Add the water and lemon zest, place in the rice cooker, close the lid, and push the Cook button. Cook for approximately 40 to 50 minutes. If the rice cooker turns to Keep Warm mode during this time, continue to cook on Keep Warm mode until cooked.

5. Transfer the artichokes to a dish and sprinkle with parsley.

6. To prepare the lemon butter sauce: melt the butter in a small saucepan, add lemon with rind and juice. Remove saucepan from heat source, and add salt and pepper to taste.

7. Let the sauce cool a bit and serve warm with artichokes.

TIP

Use any left over lemon butter sauce with steamed vegetables. Drizzle the sauce over the steamed vegetables or potatoes.

1   **lemon, use zest and juice**
3   **medium artichokes (about 8 oz each)**
3   **tbs extra virgin olive oil**
2   **tbs white wine**
2   **tbs water**
3   **tbs finely chopped fresh parsley**

LEMON BUTTER SAUCE:
¼   **cup unsalted butter**
½   **lemon, use grated rind and juice**
Salt and pepper to taste

glazed vegetables

¼ cup melted unsalted butter
½ cup hot water
3 tsp sugar
12 pearl onions, blanched
12 baby carrots, blanched
12 baby zucchinis, blanched

MENU SETTING: **QUICK COOKING**
SERVES **4**

1. In the inner cooking pan, place the butter, hot water, and sugar. Place the inner cooking pan in the rice cooker, close the lid, push the Cook button, and bring to a boil.

2. Stir in the vegetables and coat them well with the glazed butter sauce for 4 to 5 minutes. Serve the vegetables as an accompaniment for chicken, pork, fish, or beef.

assorted squash soup

MENU SETTING: **QUICK COOKING**
SERVES **4**

1. Push the Cook button of the rice cooker, and melt butter in the inner cooking pan. Sauté onion, celery, and carrot.

2. Add squash, potatoes, and chicken stock to the inner cooking pan, close the lid, and bring to a boil.

3. When the rice cooker turns to Keep Warm mode, check if potato and squash are fully cooked. If not, leave it in Keep Warm mode until fully cooked.

4. Turn off the rice cooker, take the inner cooking pan out of the rice cooker and cool enough to blend.

5. In a blender, add the vegetables and stock from the inner cooking pan. Purée well.

6. Pour the blended soup back into the inner cooking pan, place in the rice cooker, close the lid, and push the Cook button. If the rice cooker does not turn on, allow to cool, and then try again. Cover and cook until the soup is hot.

7. Add cinnamon and nutmeg, and stir well.

8. Serve with a dollop of heavy cream.

3   tbs unsalted butter
½   onion, roughly chopped
½   sprig celery, roughly chopped
1   carrot, peeled and roughly chopped
1 lb acorn squash, peeled and cut into 1- to 2-inch cubes
1 lb banana squash, peeled and cut into 1- to 2-inch cubes
1   large potato, peeled and cut into 1- to 2-inch cubes
5   cups chicken stock (use can or see recipe on page 45)
Pinch ground cinnamon
Pinch ground nutmeg
2   tbs heavy cream

steamed vegetables with dill creme sauce

1 cup water
2 red potatoes, quartered
1 cup cauliflower flowerettes
4 baby carrots
4 Brussels sprouts
1 cup zucchini, cut into 1-inch pieces
1 cup broccoli spears

DILL CREAM SAUCE:
$\frac{2}{3}$ cup mayonnaise
$\frac{1}{4}$ cup sour cream
$\frac{1}{4}$ cup milk or half & half
3 sprigs fresh dill
1 tbs lemon juice or red wine vinegar
Salt and pepper to taste

MENU SETTING: **QUICK COOKING**
SERVES **4**

1. Pour water into the inner cooking pan, set a steaming basket inside and place in the rice cooker.

2. Arrange the potatoes neatly on the steaming basket, close the lid and push the Cook button.

3. Wait for 7 to 8 minutes, and place the rest of the vegetables on the steaming basket. Continue to cook for another 15 minutes.

4. To prepare the dill cream sauce: place all ingredients into a blender and blend until all the ingredients are combined (1 to 2 minutes). Or you can mix manually.

5. Cook until the vegetables are tender, but firm. Insert a skewer in the middle of the vegetables to see the tenderness. Be careful not to make big holes.

6. Arrange on a platter and serve lukewarm with the dill sauce.

apple cider with cinnamon

4   **cups apple cider or apple juice**
4   **sticks cinnamon**
3   **whole cloves**
4   **whole all spices**

MENU SETTING: QUICK COOKING
SERVES 4

1. Place all the ingredients in the inner cooking pan and place it in the rice cooker. Close the lid and push the Cook button.

2. When the rice cooker turns to Keep Warm mode, it is ready to serve.

ginger crème brûlée

MENU SETTING: QUICK COOKING
SERVES 4

3	cups heavy cream
6	tbs sugar
1	pod vanilla, halved
2	tbs minced ginger
4	egg yolks
1	whole egg
Sugar for carmelizing	

1. Place the cream, sugar, vanilla, and ginger in the inner cooking pan. Place in the rice cooker, close the lid, and push the Cook button.

2. When the liquid starts to boil (8 to 10 minutes), turn off the rice cooker and take out the inner cooking pan. Keep covered and allow to steep for 30 minutes.

3. Strain the cream and set aside. Clean the inner cooking pan.

4. In a medium bowl, whisk the egg yolks and egg together, and slowly pour the reserved cream mixture into the eggs to combine.

5. Pour the custard into 4 ramekins and place them in the inner cooking pan with 1-inch of water. Put two ramekins at a time if all four do not fit in the rice cooker (to prevent eggs and cream from going bad, make sure to keep the remaining two ramekins in the refrigerator while cooking the first two, and bring to room temperature before use).

6. Place the inner cooking pan into the rice cooker, close the lid and push the Cook button. When the rice cooker turns to Keep Warm mode, remove the ramekins from the inner cooking pan.

7. Let cool to room temperature and then refrigerate for 30 minutes.

8. When ready to serve, sprinkle an even thin layer of sugar on top of the cream and torch to caramelize the sugar using a crème brulee torch, or place ramekins under a broiler till the sugar is caramelized.

9. Serve immediately.

DESSERT

chocolate risotto

MENU SETTING: **QUICK COOKING**
SERVES **4**

1. Push the Cook button of the rice cooker and heat the inner cooking pan. Melt the butter and cook the rice for 2 minutes, stirring until the rice is well coated in butter.

2. Meanwhile, in a separate pan, heat the milk to just below boiling point. Reduce the heat to a gentle simmer.

3. Pour in 2 cups of the heated milk over the rice in the inner cooking pan, stirring constantly with a wooden spoon for 10 minutes or until the rice has absorbed almost all the milk. Repeat with all the remaining milk, and let the rice absorb all the milk.

4. Add sugar and vanilla, and continue to cook until the rice absorbs all the liquid.

5. Stir in the chocolate and cream, and cook for about 5 minutes.

6. Serve in a dish garnished with berries and mint leaves.

4 tbs unsalted butter
2 cups (rice measuring cup) Arborio rice
$4\frac{1}{2}$ cups milk
2 tbs superfine or plain sugar
2 tsp pure vanilla extract
3 oz grated semisweet chocolate
$\frac{2}{3}$ cup heavy cream
Fresh berries for garnish
Fresh mint leaves for garnish

DESSERT

berry compote

1   cup raspberries
1   cup blueberries
1   cup strawberries, halved
1/3   cup sugar
1   tbs lemon juice
1   tbs water
1/2   tsp pure vanilla extract

VARIATION
Serve the compote over ice cream, pies, pancakes, and French toast.

MENU SETTING: **QUICK COOKING**
SERVES **4**

1. Place all the ingredients in the inner cooking pan of the rice cooker, close the lid and push the Cook button.

2. When the rice cooker turns to Keep Warm mode, take out the inner cooking pan. Cool to room temperature and serve or keep in refrigerator in tightly closed container for up to 3 days.

ABOUT THE AUTHOR: Chef Jayne E. Chang learned about Eastern and Western cooking during childhood and developed a passion for good food. Her father traveled all over the world for business and would bring his daughter along to expose her to variety of smells and tastes. Her mother comes from a long line of Yangban family, with close ties to the Joseon dynasty's royal kitchen. She taught her daughter the secret recipes of the Korean Royal Kitchen. Jayne Chang has been a chef at renowned restaurants, a restaurant owner, a restaurant consultant, food columnist, and TV food personality.

In September of 2004, Chef Jayne E. Chang opened the first Korean-American cooking school in Los Angeles pursuing her vision to bridge Korean and Pan-Asian cuisine to the mainstream American and Western societies. Chef Jayne E. Chang also saw the opportunity to make European cuisine more accessible to the Korean-American community. In the fall of 2006, the school was granted a permanent approval from the Bureau of Private Postsecondary Vocational Education (BPPVE). She envisions the school will become a true multi-cuisine melting pot, where new and old ideas, techniques and tastes can incorporate to produce a fragrant harmony of flavor.

CPCS offers year around Professional (Certificate Granting) and Recreational classes in Pan-Asian and European Culinary Arts. The school offers special series and one-day cooking classes. Chef Jayne also works as a restaurant consultant and lecturer. For further information: contact the school at 213.386.2727 or e-mail: info@cpcsla.com. The School's website is www.cpcsla.com.

Please visit our web site, www.zojirushi.com, for rice recipes and information on other quality Zojirushi products.

Rice Cooker Creations, Copyright © 2007 by Zojirushi America Corporation

Published by Silverback Books, Inc.

Text and original recipes created by Jayne Chang
Project Editor: Lisa M. Tooker
Design, Art Direction and Layout by Elizabeth Watson
Photography by Lisa Keenan
Food Stylist: Agnes (Pouke) Halpern
Prop Stylist: Carol Hacker
The Elephant Logo, Elephant and Zojirushi are registered trademarks of Zojirushi Corporation. Neuro Fuzzy is a registered trademark of Zojirushi America Corporation.

ISBN 1-59637-230-3
Printed in Korea

index